This book belongs to

_____

Caring Ninja

By Mary Nhin

Pictures by
Jelena Stupar

People always seemed upset around Caring Ninja.

His friend was running and tripped over Caring Ninja's backpack. He grazed his knee and cried.

Emotionally Intelligent Ninja was carrying a tall pile of books and walked into the door, bruising his eye.

His mom was carrying four heavy bags of groceries and one of them spilled all over the ground.

Caring Ninja told Patient Ninja all about his bad week.

Caring Ninja felt tears fill his eyes.

When Caring Ninja read a book during the week, he put it back when he was done. His brother was surprised.

When Mom went shopping, Caring Ninja went with her, and helped check the items off the list. Then, he helped to put the groceries away too. He, also, made time to help his mom tidy up the kitchen.

Thank you, Caring Ninja!

Changing the lightbulb took seconds, and Dad came down safely.

That was so easy this time! Thanks, Caring Ninja!

Caring Ninja and his friend were playing leapfrog, and there was a big muddy puddle. Caring Ninja warned his friend.

Caring Ninja loved the way it made him feel good inside to care about others. No one was cross with Caring Ninja any more. And he liked it like that!

Remembering to care could be your
secret weapon in feeling amazing inside!

Visit ninjalifehacks.tv for fun freebies!

@marynhin   @GrowGrit
#NinjaLifeHacks

Mary Nhin   Ninja Life Hacks

Ninja Life Hacks

CPSIA information can be obtained
at www.ICGtesting.com
Printed in the USA
LVHW071302060421
683577LV00009B/139